The Time Management Book

Increase your Productivity, Get Things Done Fast and boost your Effectivity within 2 Weeks incl. Productivity Planner

1. Edition

Peter L. Gardner

Contents

Introduction

Life is filled with assignments, tasks, challenges and expectations. Life's variations can be prodigious. Even the most organized person can plan their day or life right down to the last second but may encounter roadblocks that interfere with those plans. It's life. Sometimes you can get things done and other times, it's almost impossible.

What is your daily life like? Do you spend hour upon hour trying to keep a schedule or meet certain goals? How do you feel if you fail to accomplish those goals or maintain a perfect schedule? It would be nice if there was a handbook on how to successfully accomplish tasks each time. While there may not be a handbook, there are strategies that can help you progress productively and lead a progressively operative life.

To achieve proper productivity and time management, you must first have the desire to do both. Is the desire there for you? What is your motivation for wanting to get things done appropriately and on time? How is failure to meet deadlines or goals impacting your life? In many regards, people are eager to accomplish things but don't implement the necessary strategies to accomplish greatness. Effective planning is a crucial factor in time management and getting things done meritoriously.

Let's examine the necessary factors that contribute to getting things done effectively. There is no formula, but there are strategies. There are no steps, but there are practices that may help improve the way you get things done. To produce and live effectively, you must establish a solid foundation for sustainment.

A successful foundation begins with you. You should identify and understand your potential to contribute and succeed in everything you attempt. Secondly, you should realize the importance of being productive in life. Finally, you should determine if your efforts are aligned with your potential in being productive.

You may be glad to know that there is an effective system that helps with getting things done. There is not a single system, but one for almost every facet of life. Which system works best for you? You may not immediately have an answer to this question if you're not acquainted with either or all systems. Your primary objective should be to identify the system that best adapts to your lifestyle. The positive aspect is that there is a system for almost every lifestyle, including yours. The guide aims to assist you with identifying and implementing the system that motivates and enables you to effectively utilize the time you time, be more productive and get things done efficiently.

Getting things done on time and in an efficient manner provides a sense of relief. Understanding the process or knowing that you are taking the proper steps to achieve a goal or accomplish a task helps to reduce a sense of overwhelm that you may feel otherwise. There is an association among your purpose, motivation and effectiveness in life. All these factors work together in one way or another to help you achieve most of the things you set out to do.

Remove the inconveniences of stress or overwhelm in your life by zoning in on the most effective system in getting things done in your life. If you can't produce or manage your time appropriately can interfere with various avenues of life. This guide is designed to help you take control of the areas in your life that are less organized and possibly causing you to experience undue stress and chaos.

The Importance of Getting Things Done

Getting things done efficiently and appropriately is important. It is so essential, the most beneficial mindset is to simply do what is required to achieve the objective. Yes. That's the best mindset but not always the easiest. It requires energy, means and time management to do things in consideration of the time. Let's face it, no two days are the same and you may feel like you're capable of building an empire on Monday but have no idea where to start on Tuesday.

You've likely experienced the ups and downs of being productive. The feeling of completion exists when you can cross one or more items off your waiting to do list is a refreshing that most wish to experience every day. You will find that completing the smallest task leads you to feel accomplished and give you the necessary motivation to proceed to the next item on the list. It's as if the completion of one little thing sets off a fire within you and before you know it, you've burned through your entire "to do" list.

It's normal to feel stuck in a mood where it seems you can't get anything done. Most people overthink the process of what's next to do instead of progressing forward without thought. Get up and get things done, regardless of how small they are. Not only does it help you accomplish necessary things, but it helps you to feel better about yourself and your progress.

What's next in your mental or actual recipe of things to do? Where will you start? Have you devised a plan or strategy to realize these things effectively? Is your mind running away with thoughts of the things that await your attention and you have not the slightest clue why you aren't chopping away at them? If so, examine your system and reorganize your life today. If your brain is plagued with to-do items- your planning board, calendar or scheduling system should reflect those items.

Writing it down and getting it done is always a great place to start, mentally. A mental approach is the initial phase of making things happen in real time.

Consider these factors.

A chaotic life will likely result in a chaotic thought process.

Work on gaining clarity in the beginning. Clear your schedule of one item at a time. You could eliminate multiple "tasks" without feeling overwhelmed. Most importantly, kill the chaos.

Your vison can be easily obstructed by lack of understanding.

People often create lists of things to do with little clarity about how these things need or can be accomplished. Identify the start and end to each task you take on. During those moments that you find it difficult to complete a task, ask yourself what the completed task looks like. Think about what it really means to be done with that particular thing. If you can't see the end-result, you'll have difficulty reaching the end.

Clear your mind.

It's great if you can consistently rely on your memory or recall whatever tasks you have to complete. But it's better to use your mind for thinking and not storage. Clutter begins to feel your head when you try to keep every little thing in mind that you wish to accomplish. Again, write those things down. Attempting to mentally juggle multiple thoughts or tasks can lead to stress or overwhelm. Organize a to-do list on paper or an electronic device.

Projects vs. tasks, know the difference.

Understand that projects don't belong on a task list. This list should consist of items that can be accomplished over a short period of time. A task may take as little as an hour or as long as a day to complete, but anything that takes much longer, is most likely a project. Adding projects to your tasks list is an automatic red flag. It creates room for chaos, doubt and failure. Your goal is to get things done effectively and it begins by knowing what category those things fall under.

Another essential element of getting things done is proper execution planning. Planning sounds intimidating to a procrastinator and is greatly affected by the amount of time there is to get things done. You may consider scheduling as a type of planning, and it is similar in that it's short-term. While it is appropriate to think strategy as a long-term association of planning.

Planning and Its Impact on Getting Things Done

Short-term: planning in the short-term is essential in that it allows everyday progress to be achieved. This is usually acquired by basic management of tasks, and highlighting useful application. This is a valuable contribution to being effective in getting things done. Proper short-term planning can eliminate failure, passive conflicts ad doubt if you execute short-term planning.

Long-term: planning in the long-term is a calculated approach. The goal is to achieve viable success, but meager planning (long-term) might possibly cause demise in the attempt to get things done.

The point is, quality planning is a primary leader of getting things done.

The Values of Strategic Planning

There are some underlying values that should be observed in every process of the planning phase (short and long-term):

Decide on the resolve: plans are not made to be the resolve but instead the means to the resolve. Unbelievable to some, it is common to mistake end for the resolve.

Assess the evidence: the foundation on which your plans are built must be stable. This requires the collection of valuable information and careful alignment with your strategies. Any evidence that fails to support the ability to get things done should be eliminated.

Categorize dependencies: Does carrying out your plans depend on other people or things? Are the plans of others in your circle interfering with your ability to get things done? Categorize the dependencies and move forward with eliminating them.

Is Procrastination Effecting Your Ability to Get Things Done

Procrastination is a life encounter that almost everyone has a head-on collision with at some point. In almost every instance, people vow to not procrastinate on that next task, project or important assignment. It is crucial to have clarity on what procrastination really is before you can overcome or stop it.

Procrastination takes place when one is unable to manage their behavior in regards to accomplishing something. It's the moment when you know what needs or should be done but do the opposite to better manage self-control. In almost every occurrence, procrastination happens inadvertently. People realize it isn't good to procrastinate and desire to stop but irrational thinking makes it hard to do so.

Patterns of Procrastination

Procrastination takes place in various ways. It can have an impact on various aspects of your life. Here are a few typical patterns of procrastination:

- Surfing the web or social media platforms instead of working to get things done

- Consistently delaying starting a task until hours before it is to be completed

- Desiring to begin a new constructive habit, like healthy eating, working out, or budgeting, but consistently putting it off and promising yourself to start it soon

- Desiring to begin work on a task or launch a new business, but spend too much time searching memes, inspirational quotes and other information that has no impact on actually completing the task

Procrastination can be an intricate occurrence, as it can be experienced differently among various individuals.

The Procrastination Wheel

Procrastination is a cycle that can and needs to be broken. Begin by identifying and understanding the phases of procrastination.

Procrastination Phases

The phases of procrastination are simple. The *motivation* to get things done is often supported by the *belief* that you can accomplish the task. You realize the *importance* of completion but can sometimes confuse mental *spontaneity* with physical action, which quickly leads to the *delay* of achieving a goal in a timely manner. It's a viscous cycle that happens to almost everyone.

The Procrastination Cycle: It's the wheel that keeps spinning but never reaches its destination of completion.

While each of the preceding factors is connected to procrastination, it is critical to observe that procrastination exists in almost all categories of populations, classifying it as a highly recognized behaviors of the human race.

Identifying Habits that Discourage Productivity

Procrastination doesn't have to dictate your life or ability to get things done. Armed with the right knowledge, you can defeat it and move forward being the productive person you desire to be. To overcome it, you must first identify the habits that destructively impact productivity.

As you continue reading, observe the habits and make a mental note of those habits that occur often in your attempt to get things done. Think clearly and be honest with yourself about those habits that you notice occurring in your daily life. Taking careful notes helps to later reference them for clear examination and devising steps to overcome your habits of procrastination. The more you understand about the reasons behind your procrastination, the less challenges you'll face when attempting to stop the negative habit.

Below are a few habits that contribute to procrastination:

1. Fear of Not Being Successful

In most cases, the biggest factor in procrastination is a person's fear of not succeeding. Simply put, they're afraid they'll fail at what needs to be done. If the fear of not succeeding lurks, it leads you to withdraw from the act of attempting the task. Because not trying at a thing, prevents you from succeeding at it. Some would argue the idea that not trying is parallel to not succeeding.

Procrastination is like a blanket of comfort when the thought of not succeeding invades your thought process. It's like an armour of protection intended to help you feel safe and free of failure.

To Overcome This: Acknowledge and agree that not succeeding at something isn't fatal. Most errors can be corrected, and second chances are an option. Never set out to do something assuming you'll fail. However, it's important to understand that mistakes are common.

Condition you mind to comprehend that if you fail to attempt to try and do something, it's worse than trying and not succeeding. Attempting presents the opportunity to learn from any errors that may occur. Deciding to not try is an automatic fail because you have nothing to learn or grow from in the first place.

2. Hunger for Perfection

People who are self-proclaimed perfectionist have an issue with not succeeding at something. This leads them to delay starting a task if they aren't sure they'll be perfect at it. They seek ultimate and complete satisfaction in all they do. This is a huge issue when attempting new task or taking a different approach to something familiar. Because in their mind, they will be concerned about a less than perfect outcome. It's ideal to want to do a good job at whatever you do, but to obsess over it or seek perfection. Striving to be perfect at everything leads to procrastination because it convinces you to not attempt to do something until you are sure you'll be perfect at it. This is almost like the fear of not succeeding, except in that case, you fear that you won't meet success in your attempt but here, you have high expectations that you fear you won't meet.

To Overcome This: Try your best and accept the outcome. Realize that there is no perfect way to do a thing, especially when it is based on the opinions of others.

3. Lack of Energy

It's understandable that having little to no energy would cause procrastination. This leads a person to not feeling up to the task in most cases. This occurs often in people who lead a less than vigorous lifestyle. It could be too little sleep or exercise, or poor eating habits. All these factors could make you feel drained and low on energy, which makes it difficult for you to move and realize your potential. This pattern is easily identifiable and just as easy to correct.

To Overcome This: Begin practicing healthier habits. Adjust your sleep habits, set your body in motion to move around more, and eat a nutritious diet. You can research the numerous resources to find options that are best for your lifestyle. You likely know what is required in order to pursue a healthier way of life. If your life is aligned with the right actions but you still struggle with low energy, seek medical advice.

4. Inability to Remain Focused

If you have issues focusing or remaining focused, it could lead to procrastination. Failure to remain focused is often brought on by lack of direction or guidance. They feel they have no purpose or are not tapped in to their goals. If there is nothing in life that you are aiming to do or complete, you feel lost in life and find it difficult to concentrate or emphasize the things that need to be done.

To Overcome This: Set reachable goals. It's vital that you set standards that motivate you to be proactive, but not too high. Setting them too high could result in failure, which doesn't motivate you at all.

It is essential that you have clarity in the patterns or habits that lead to procrastination. Identify the patterns that exist in your life and exercise the steps to overcome them.

Procrastination Triggers

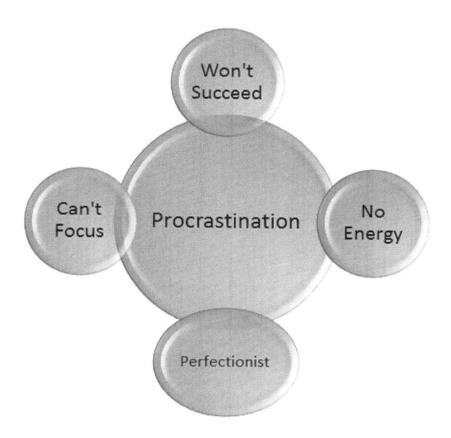

Tips to Getting Things Done Effectively

Regardless of all you do, there always seem to be something left undone. There is always room for more hours in the day. However, if you're not good at time management or have issues with procrastination, you could benefit from a few tips on getting things done effectively.

You should begin by determining what factors interfere with you being productive regarding your list of things to do. Sometimes, there may be nothing you could have done differently. Most often than not, it's a lack of focus, or attention to detail that slowed you down. Whatever the culprit may be, there are ways to improve your approach to getting things done.

Have you ever heard someone say that they never seem to finish one thing or get things done? Sure you have. You may have said this very thing yourself recently. Once you develop a productive system, it becomes easier to wipe out your to-do list. Unfortunately, many people give up and stop trying to get things done. They live with the assumption that they're awful at organizing or completing tasks. The people you admire so much because of their ability to produce quality returns on their attempts are definitely utilizing a systematic approach.

You have the ability to get things done if you simply will yourself to do it. Stop watching others and find your own way to make things happen. Following are tips that may assist in your efforts to increase the efficiency in your attempt to be more productive.

➤ **It may be listed but it doesn't HAVE to be done.** Sometimes you overextend yourself. Your lists may easily consists of things that you want to get done and in writing them down, you hastily add too many things to be done in too little time. Be respectful of all you have going on. Don't beat yourself up if something needs to be put off until next week or even next month.

➤ **Keep a "You" list**. It's simple. Make sure your list consists of things that YOU need done. Many times, we give others the power to abuse our time. Sometimes, simply tell them that it's not the best time. Add the things that you need done for yourself to your priority folder. You may find that you're more eager to complete tasks that help you achieve those things that you need done.

➤ **Lose site of the cool guys.** How many times have you added something to your list of things do just because you've noticed someone else doing it and you thought it would be a cool thing to try? Probably more than once if you're like most people. It's a typical trend but not a good one to follow. Only add essential items to your task list. Be certain there on there for the right reasons.

➤ **Delay is not defeat.** Don't feel defeated if you need to create an extended list. This list will be compiled of tasks or projects that you need to achieve later in the month or year. They may be big or large. It could be something that you need to collect certain material for or increase your knowledge about doing that particular task. Delay tasks that you lack the means or knowledge to complete at the moment. Delay is not defeat.

Before you attempt to tackle certain tasks, ask yourself these questions:

1. Are you dedicated to your purpose of completing things fully? _____

2. Do you understand everything associated with completing the task? _____

3. Is time an obstacle that's presenting delay? ____

4. What does completing the task mean to you? ____

5. Do you have the energy to complete the task successfully? ____

6. Are you doing this because you want or because someone else wants you too? ____

7. How long is your to-do list? __

8. Is there one or more tasks in your planner that you need assistance with? ____

9. Are you armed with the necessary materials to complete the task? ____

10. What will happen if you fail to complete the entire list? ____

Asking yourself the above questions helps you to

gain clarity and put things into perspective. Always approach tasks with a clear mind. Brain fog easily disrupts the ability to be productive when attempting to get things done effectively.

The Effective Rotation of Getting Things Done

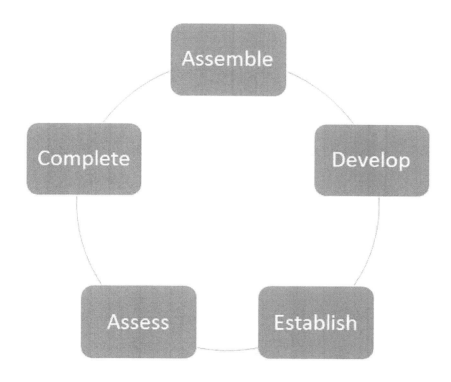

Phase 1: *Assemble* all materials and information necessary to finish whatever you have started.

Phase 2: *Develop* a plan to make your attempt most effective.

Phase 3: *Establish* a routine to make your effort most effective.

Phase 4: *Assess* your work to ensure that you have done everything correctly.

Phase 5: Mark the task *Complete* and remove it from your list of things-to-do.

When applied correctly, this is an effective cycle to get things done.

End the Running Late Cycle

Are you one of those people that can't seem to arrive anywhere on time? It's okay if you are. There are so many others out there just like you. It's as if you're destined to be late, no matter how far in advance you prepare to reach your destination. This is such a common occurrence that it's almost disregarded. However, being on time is important in many instances. Failure to arrive at a place at the time expected could eventually have negative consequences.

Ask yourself what prevents you from reaching your destination on time? If it's something that happens every blue moon, there's no reason for concern. But if you're the habitual late arriver, you should try to end the "running late cycle now. It may sound like a trial, but it's doable with a little effort and some determination. You may even think that it's no big deal that you're late but consider the feelings of others. At times, you failing to arrive as expected could wreak havoc on plans that others have.

Most people who are consistently behind on time or running late for appointments are doing so because they disregard time or never prepare to leave in time. In any regard, they give excuses similar to the ones that follow, which are not always true.

- Traffic was hectic
- My GPS took me the wrong way
- My alarm didn't go off
- There was an emergency

- I lost track of time

- I thought we were meeting later

- I went to the wrong address

- The babysitter was late (I couldn't find a sitter)

While many of the above can easily happen, they sometimes happen to the same person ALL the time. It's time to get serious and end the cycle to running late. You will notice that people will value your time more if you begin to value their time.

Here are a few suggestions to help you arrive to your next appointment on time:

- Prepare for the appointment the day before

- Leave home 30 minutes earlier than necessary

- Set an alarm to alert you when you should be going out the door

- Map your route to new places the day before

- Suggest someone else pick you up to ensure you get there on time

Running late can cause issues for students, athletes and employees. It's important to develop healthy habits for being on time early in life. Once you start running late for things, it's difficult to stop. Train your mind to be responsible for the time you take from others and you'll be more conducive to being punctual to places where your arrival is anticipated.

The Meaning of Productivity

Productivity is simple to explain and even simpler to understand. Aligned with the dictionary's definition, it is the act of completing a task successfully. People are productive on their jobs, in educational pursuit, with family, and in social settings. Productivity is important at almost every level of life. It is taught at a very young age, as parents work with little ones to take baby steps, write their alphabets, learn their shapes and colors and other similar teachings. Kids who learn to do these things early are usually productive in playgroups and the classroom.

Is your inability to be productive interfering with certain areas of your life? It's easy to be disrupted because you can't excel at the level expected by yourself or others. If you are not productive due to lack of effort, the matter needs personal attention. If you are not productive due to poor planning, training, or knowledge, there are positive strategies or methods that can help you improve in that area. Your ability to produce positively has a huge impact on various areas of your life.

Here are a few ways that quality productivity will benefit you in life:

You study and obtain good grades	Possibly gain awards and promotions
You work hard to learn plays	Possibly gain a starting position on the team
You take extra courses to learn more about your job	Possibly gain a team leader position or promotion
You are attentive and follow instructions	Possibly succeed at completing the task correctly on the first try
You give it a try even if you are unsure that you can do it	You accomplish the task at first try or acquire valuable information to help you get it done the next time around

The above are a few common examples of ways that productivity leads to positive events in life. The effort is simple, but the outcome can be tremendous. Most people think of work when the word productivity is mentioned. While the term does apply to work, it applies to other faculties of your existence also.

How do you respond to these questions?

Are you leading a less than productive life?

Do you wish that you were more productive on your job, school, or at home?

Is a lack of productivity impacting your happiness?

Are you often reprimanded because you don't produce as you should on the job or at school?

Do you refrain from attempting certain tasks because you fear you won't produce appropriately?

If your answer is YES to at least two of the previous questions, continue on and discover how your productivity levels can become more efficient.

Strategies for Effective Productivity

Even the most productive person can learn a few things about improving their strategies and becoming better at certain things. There is no science to learning to be more productive but when implemented correctly, the right strategies can program the scale for productivity in almost everything you do. The key is to study and implement these strategies consistently. You may notice that when you don't practice these steps, your productivity levels will drop. If important enough, you will strive to make every effort to succeed at leading a productive life.

What happens if you are not productive in school, work, or at home? There are multiple things that can occur if you aren't productive in these places. Before things get too far behind, put forth an effort to improve your productivity and experience the positive benefits they bring to your life.

The Non-productivity Stress Impact

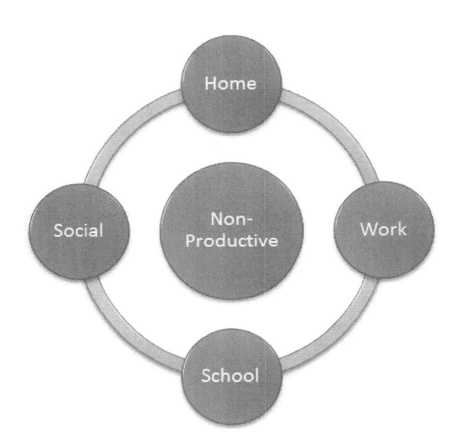

If you continue to be non-productive, you may experience stressors like below:

- A stressful home life

- Incomplete feelings and emotions

- Disconnect among close family

- Illness or unhealthy habits

- Failure to progress in the workplace

- Strained relationship with co-workers

- Inability to connect with your social circle

Productiveness should not be discounted as a little factor. It's essential to pay close attention to the areas where you are not producing as you should. There could be mental interferences that prevent you from performing satisfactorily in certain areas. If you're unable to think properly due to changing stages in life, at home, at work or other places, remove yourself from projects until you can overcome the issues you're facing. However, if there are no interferences, work diligently to implement the necessary strategies for productivity and begin to enjoy a better life immediately.

Productivity Ideas

Manage Your Time Wisely

Learning to manage your time effectively is a solid tool for being productive. Utilize the time you have effectively. Make and keep a schedule of tasks. Electronic calendars are beneficial in helping you to stay organized and not miss appointments. Remember that time is valuable and once it's wasted, you can't get it back.

Align Tasks with Skillsets

It's easy to assign tasks based on available bodies. Consider only accepting those tasks for which you are adequately skilled at achieving. It won't help to agree to do a thing just because no one else wants to do it, especially if you're unsure of how to do what you're signing up for. Only take on tasks of which you are familiar or know how to accomplish.

Preparation

To be productive, you need to be prepared and have knowledge of what you're tasked to do. Preparation can help you acquire the necessary knowledge and skills to get things done efficiently. Make certain that you are knowledgeable of the requirements necessary to be productive at what you're attempting. You will find that being prepared for certain things will help you achieve efficiency in productivity.

Attention to Detail

You must be attentive to detail to successfully complete tasks. Productivity requires accomplishing the little things, just as well as the little things. Not overlooking the small details can help you produce efficiently in almost every area of life.

Track Your Progress

Keep notes of those capacities that need improvement. If you keep track of the areas in which you need improvement, you will be prompted to study and work towards improving them. Productivity may not occur in that area instantly, but as time advances, you'll improve at it and begin positive production.

Steps to Being More Productive

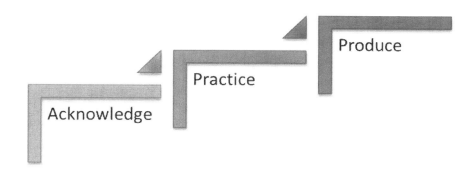

These are the primary steps to improving your productivity.

1. Acknowledge the areas in which you need improvement.

2. Practice methods to help you improve in those areas.

3. Produce quality results when implementing what you learned in practice.

Tips to Improve Daily Productivity

Are you convinced that you could be more productive at work, school, or at home? Do you spend time each day trying to think of ways you can be more productive? Being productive provides a feeling of completion in many people. It's almost like a self-esteem booster. Knowing that you are productive in life gives you the confidence you need to try new things and achieve at doing them.

There are several ways to improve your level of productivity in almost every regard. Imagine the positive benefits associated with positive production. They are tremendous and bring great rewards to life as you know it. You may not realize it, but it's possible that you are your biggest distraction in life. Your personality, indecisiveness, lack of organization, and inability to commit could be among the many distractions that prevent you from being a productive person.

These tips may help to improve your daily productivity:

1. Stop delaying your tasks awaiting the perfect time. By now, you must realize that there are no perfect times. You must act immediately and approach the tasks with positive energy.

2. Check and respond to emails in the afternoon and utilize the morning hours to work on tasks because you likely have more energy during this time.

3. Write down your goals or tasks and visit the list daily to keep them on your mind. Commit to complete at least one goal or task each week.

4. Cancel your favorite reality television episodes. If reality television is your thing, you're likely spending too much time trying things the wrong way. These shows lead you to think unrealistically. It's often never as easy to achieve a big goal as the reality stars make it seem.

5. Eliminate the naysayers. You should rid your environment and life of anyone who interjects negativity into your life. Surround yourself with people who support you and your efforts. Negativity will drain you of your positive energy and good intentions.

6. Find and stick to a routine that works. If you have developed a routine that results in you being productive in some areas of life, stick to it. Don't change what's working for you.

7. Rise early. Don't spend too many hours of your morning in bed thinking about all the things that await you. Leap out of bed early and get started on those tasks. Working towards certain tasks earlier in the day allows you to complete them and free up time for you to work on additional tasks later in the day.

8. Declutter. Remove any excessive clutter from your home, room, office or brain. Productivity isn't easy in a cluttered environment. The junk that invades your space could be preventing you from achieving goals or completing certain tasks.

9. Meet less. Meetings are great for planning but there's no need to schedule a meeting for every phase of a project. Be clear on the instructions at the initial meeting, schedule a progress meeting half-way through the project, make the necessary adjustments and schedule a final meeting to close the project out. Scheduling too many meetings could slow down progression of the project, which could result in non-productive results.

10. Turn them down. You shouldn't accept every task introduced to you. You may not have time or availability to approach a task. Turn it down to prevent taking on too much. When you feel overwhelmed with things to do, you will probably not do any of the items on your list well.

11. Spread the joy. Everything doesn't have to be done by you. Feeling overwhelmed is normal. If you think a project will result in better success if you enlist others to assist, do it. It takes nothing away from you to ask for assistance. Aim to accomplish the task. No one said that you must do it all alone.

12. Exercise. This may seem like a stretch but you will be both mentally and physically replenished. Exercise removes the fog from your brain and increases energy levels. If you are thinking clearly and have high levels of energy, you can complete almost any task successfully.

13. Take a break. You should schedule 15-20 minute breaks for every three hours you work towards a personal goal or project. After about six hours, call it a day until your next attempt. Working at something consistently without sufficient breaks can cause you to become fatigued or burned out in the process. Mini-breaks keep you alert and focused on your goal.

14. List all the things you know you should avoid. You should write out those things that you wish to avoid. These may be things that you're not good at doing or just don't like at all. It can be challenging to complete tasks when you are forced to do things you have no knowledge of or hate doing. Keeping a list of these things reminds you not to engage in or accept tasks that involve the things you don't care for or have difficulty doing.

15. First impressions are ideal for tasks. IF you take the right approach, utilize your time wisely, and are organized when you approach the task, you may succeed the first time. This is great motivation and you may be inclined to work on similar projects in the future.

Experiencing daily productivity may lead to a productive life overall. If you are producing quality results at work, school, or other areas, chances increase for you to positively impact others and improve in the area of productivity.

End Procrastination and Live Productively

Procrastination could be keeping you from your greatest potential in life. As a procrastinator, you put off those things that are vital to you and others. You have the best intentions but consistently delaying the start of something could result in a disastrous or non-productive result. Sometimes, others rely on you to get things done but because procrastinating is a habit, you can't always meet your obligation.

- At what point do you admit that procrastination is a problem and you need guidance?

- How much of your life is negatively impacted by your procrastination?

- Has procrastination caused you to lose money or important jobs?

- Are you constantly saying you'll start the project today, and once night arrives, the project hasn't been started?

- Is it hard for you to just get started on a project or task?

Answering yes to at least two of the above questions may mean that you're a serious procrastinator. You can put an end to this ineffective way of life and begin to live a productive life very soon. It's almost impossible to be a procrastinator and lead a productive life.

Understanding what is causing you to procrastinate is equally as important as ending the habit. The list is endless but for most, it's a handful of the same excuses or reasons that prevent them from getting things done.

Procrastinators are typically associated with claiming that they are:

- Always busy
- Always tired
- Broke
- Stressed
- Afraid of the risks
- Inexperienced
- Not sure
- Not interested

Though these may sometimes be plausible reasons, they can be big factors in the procrastination cycle. If a person seems to always produce an excuse such as one of the previous, they are probably procrastinating.

Tactics to End Procrastination and Produce More Effectively.

1. **Write the task down and set a deadline for completion.** A task that has no completion date can be delayed indefinitely.

2. **Divide the tasks into parts**. This is ideal for larger tasks. Break it down and work at it day by day or every other day. The objective is to not become overwhelmed by big tasks and leave it unaccomplished. You can learn as you go for projects that you are not entirely familiar

with or enlist the help of someone that has knowledge of what you're attempting to do.

3. **Imagine how completion feels.** Allow your mind to wonder to the moment you complete the task. Imagine how relieved and happy you'll feel that you were able to get it done in time and correctly. Play it out in your mind how others will benefit from your ability to produce quality results.

4. **Freeze fear.** Don't allow fear to prevent you from trying. Concentrate on the result you wish to achieve. Now, imagine the outcome if you don't attempt to complete the task because you were afraid of the challenge. It's important to freeze fear and give it your all when trying anything in life.

5. **Pick your team.** You need a team of positive people in your life. This team will rally around you to give you support and encouragement when necessary. They are charged with holding you accountable. This category of individuals should be driven and understand that you need to overcome your habit of procrastination.

6. **Celebrate your achievements.** It is okay to tell yourself "good job" when you accomplish a goal or complete a task. Knowing that you will celebrate at the end of a productive outcome may make you work harder to accomplish tasks that you start.

7. **Get uncomfortable.** Don't only attempt those things or tasks that you are comfortable doing. Choose at least one tasks per month that makes you uncomfortable. These are the things that remind you that you're capable of doing anything you put your mind to as long as you try.

If you are a procrastinator, don't add others like you to important tasks. It may lead to roadblocks during the path of the project. Work on yourself to remove the habit of procrastination. You will likely wake each day with more motivation when the tasks of yesterday, last week, or last month aren't occupying your mind. Incomplete tasks linger in the mind for a long time, which interferes with the successful completion of new or upcoming tasks.

Remember these steps when you are trying to end procrastination:

1. Identify the reasons that cause you to procrastinate.

2. Take things into your capable hands and work towards the goal or task each day. A few minutes is all it takes.

3. Make a schedule of days and times to work towards your goal.

4. Don't be down on yourself if you can't meet your daily goals. There's always tomorrow.

5. Remind yourself how good it felt the last time you started and completed a task on time without procrastinating.

Effective Use of Time at Work

The saying that "time is of the essence" definitely applies to the workplace. You should practice being on time and proper utilization of time at work. There are very few jobs that don't stress the importance of time management. If this type job exists, you probably don't have it. Time management is vital for entry and upper level employees. Regardless of your job title, you should be managing your time effectively in order to be a productive employee.

Time management can be described as the careful planning of your day to create a productive schedule. It is the attempt to accomplish tasks or assignments in a manner that gives careful regard to the time you have available vs. the time required for task completion.

Enhancing the management of work time permits you to improve performance and reach your objectives with little effort but a more realistic approach. If efficient management of time is unaccounted for, it could lead to:

- Unmet deadlines and missed appointments
- Inability to focus
- Absence of commitment or professionalism
- Barren work results
- Unnecessary stress

The Importance of Executing Your Time Wisely at Work

In the competitive industries of today, you can achieve a lot by being aware of the skills it takes to manage your calendar. It is good practice to spend time in a way that is most beneficial to you and your happiness, especially in the workplace.

These are the positive factors of efficient time management in your career.

Complete work on time.

Designating a set time frame to work on tasks will motivate you to complete them on schedule. You will also learn to take control of your assignments and manage them more efficiently. Once you set your tasks to a schedule, your brain gets onboard and motivates you to adhere to the schedule and complete the tasks within the time you've allotted. Your workload is less stressful if you are adapted to a schedule and practice time management.

Deliver quality end-results.

If you work within a managed time schedule, you can produce quality end-results in the workplace. Because you are organized and acknowledge the time you have available as work-related, you will have ample time to complete the assignment and not feel rushed to meet the deadline. This will enhance the end-result because you allowed yourself the proper amount of time to do the job.

Increased productivity.

Managing your time appropriately will definitely help you to improve your productivity in the workplace. You will sometimes complete tasks early, which allows time for you to check over your work for errors. Submitting quality work is a plus in the workplace, because it removes the need for other employees to spend quality time correcting your errors.

Eliminates procrastination.

Wise management of your availability, you will complete things at the time planned, regardless. This eliminates the destructive habit of procrastination. You strive to manage your time appropriately in order to spend quality time producing quality work. Saving a large task till the last minute could lead to a rushed job that results in poor quality. Incorporating time management strategies in the workplace puts you in a good place, as you implement smart strategies to complete difficult tasks.

Stress-free days.

You will find that cramming tasks into very little time could cause significant amounts of stress. Most people perform poorly when influenced by stress. You won't be productive if you are feeling overwhelmed or stressed. It can also cause you to feel anxious or overworked, which may result in serious health issues. Employees who practice quality management of time often enjoy stress-free work days and produce great quality work.

Life is better in other areas.

If you practice healthy management of your time at work, you will begin to experience greatness throughout various aspects of life. If you are succeeding at work, your social, family, and active life will benefit. If your work projects are on target and you're not behind in the workplace, you'll feel reassured and comfortable in areas outside of work.

Increased opportunities at work.

Completing tasks and assignments on time will get you noticed at work. Your superiors will note it and begin to recommend you for more projects and eventually, job advancement opportunities. This is an ideal of example of the saying, "it pays to be punctual" because a promotion could mean greater pay.

Negative Time Management Habits in the Workplace

- Arriving to work later than scheduled to do so
- Missing important meetings
- Waiting too late to begin working towards a deadline
- Not asking questions that could help you complete a job successfully
- Leaving work earlier than scheduled
- Not maintaining a calendar of open work projects that require your attention

Positive Time Management Habits in the Workplace

- Arriving to work earlier than scheduled
- Confirming meeting times and arriving on time and on the scheduled day
- Establishing a timeline for working on a project towards the deadline
- Asking vital questions to help you complete a task without delay
- Maintaining a calendar of pending tasks

Tips to Maximize the Utilization of Time in Your Career

Do you feel that your job is suffering or at risk because you aren't managing your time appropriately? Workplace competition is on the rise and your job is never safe as an employee. There are hundreds of others waiting on you to fail at the position. Your goal should be to remain productive and improve your time management skills wherever necessary.

The tips that follow can help you improve time management in your career.

1. **Plan effectively**. Careful management of time requires proper planning. This doesn't require a strict timeline, but a scheduled plan for you to follow in your daily duties. This enables you to make wise choices when attempting to complete work projects. If you plan effectively, you can strategize your work efforts and have time to focus on other tasks also.

2. **Prioritize tasks**. If you have multiple tasks at work, prioritize them efficiently. Separate the large and important tasks from the small and unimportant tasks. Although unimportant, the small tasks must be accomplished also. Utilize tools that allow you to strategize how you will approach each task, small or large.

3. **Forget multitasking.** Forget what you've been told, multitasking is not always the best approach. When juggling multiple tasks, you may accomplish nothing at all. Designate a single task and work diligently to complete it. Once completed, move to the next task on your list. This allows you to focus on a single task without being concerned with another one that you started earlier but didn't complete.

4. **Dodge the distractions.** Life is filled with distractions, especially in the workplace. There is always the chatty co-worker in the cubicle next to yours, the smell of coffee lingering from the breakroom, or the irresistible urge to surf social media. Don't allow distractions such as these to occupy your time. They will cause you to fall behind on your work and easily lose track of what needs to be done. After a while, it becomes a cycle and your work productivity is tarnished. Instead, talk with the chatty co-worker during your break, sign out of all social media pages until after work hours and grab coffee before work and during breaks.

5. **Establish unique break times**. Don't take your breaks because everyone else does if possible. If break isn't mandatory at a certain time, take your break when fewer people are doing so. This gives you time to relax your mind and not become consumed with break room conversation that can easily carry over into regular work hours. Be the odd man out and eat lunch alone sometimes. Spend this time clearing your mind and preparing to return to work and capitalize on the time you have to complete important tasks.

Time Management in School

There always seem to never be enough time in the day, especially for students. People usually say that life is easy for students because most of them have nothing to do but study and attend class. Failure to do those things effectively, can make life extremely stressful and challenging in more ways than one. From elementary school to college, it is necessary for students to develop quality skills to help them manage their time. Doing so helps them plan for almost everything that awaits them ahead.

Are you a student that struggles to get things done in a timely manner?

Do you seem to always cram for upcoming tests?

Are your class notes less than organized or you constantly need to borrow notes from fellow students?

Do you miss a class or two almost weekly or every other week?

Do you have trouble waking on time for your morning or afternoon classes?

Do you fail to complete and turn in assignments on time?

It is understandable that students may experience complications with at least one of the issues stated above, occasionally. Students that find themselves in some of the above scenarios often, you should employ strategies to improve your time management. Leading you to be a more productive student could be the outcome.

Maximize Effective Use of Your Time as a Student

Students that struggle with time management will eventually endure stress and extreme overwhelm. These factors often lead to failing grades, low self-esteem, and feelings of defeat. You are not predetermined to continue along this path. There are methods to help students and their support system develop the necessary approach to managing their time more effectively.

Once you learn to manage your time efficiently, life may improve. Your approach to school, classes, and school in general will change drastically. There are great benefits to developing skills that help you become more aware of time as a student.

The Benefits

- Students acquire improved organizational skills
- Students experience increased confidence
- Students obtain information more meritoriously
- Students experience less school associated stress
- Students become more disciplined

Negative Time Management Habits of Students

- Failure to get enough sleep the night before class or exams

- Spending too much time cramming for a test hours before it is scheduled

- Poor note taking skills because you were late to class

- Failure to attend all classes and rush to collect notes from other students who attended regularly

- Not allowing enough time to eat balanced meals-which keep you energetic and alert throughout the day

Positive Time Management Habits of Students

- Get at least 6-8 hours of rest prior to testing

- Study for exams daily instead of last-minute cramming

- Take quality notes in each class

- Attend each class on your schedule unless ill or other emergencies arise

- Lead a healthy lifestyle that includes exercise and good eating habits

Students often misconceive the importance of what they consider little things such as attending class, quality note taking, and staying for the entire class. Once they realize that these are major factors in being a successful student, it may be too late.

Tips to Improve Time Management in School

These tips and exercises when applied correctly, may help students improve grades and reduce stress levels while studying.

1. **Create a principal schedule**. Make a primary schedule that you can utilize to section off specific hours to study, complete projects, or participate in study sessions. This helps you to prioritize school work and develop structure that keeps you ahead in class and possibly with your grades. Use highlighters to separate subjects to make the schedule readable.

2. **Establish an agenda.** Create the agenda to record recurring and non-recurring assignments and the dates they are due. Also add extra-curricular activities such as television and social media time to this agenda. Following the agenda as it is printed prevents you from spending more time than you should on social media or watching television.

3. **Trash distractions.** Distractions seem to be in every corner when you're a student. Mobile devices, emails, friends, and active social circles are only a select few of the distractors that students face. However, it's important to stick to the agenda and to begin, you need to get rid of any distractions around you and avoid any that may occur during the process. Power off your mobile device and log out of social media accounts during class and study time. It's okay to listen to music that motivates you when studying if necessary, but don't become

more consumed with the music that your studies. Some students find music distracting, while others find that it helps them to remain focused or concentrate on their work.

4. **Develop a blueprint for study times**. Students who establish goals for their study times benefit greatly. Write down how many chapters you plan to study, how many questions you want to answer correctly before moving on to another section, and how much time you want to dedicate to each subject daily. Use the agenda and principal schedule to assist with the plan development.

5. **Tackle assignments as they are given.** This doesn't mean that you should complete your assignment the day it's given. It does suggest that you begin working towards completion early on. For instance, once you get an assignment, begin collecting material or conducting research that will help you complete it successfully. You may also consider reading over the assignment once you are home to ensure you have a clear understanding. This prevents you from being confused days before it's due and possibly needing help that may be difficult to get at that time.

6. **Plan out the project**. It helps to have a plan for almost all of life's tasks, but especially for class assignments. This works great with large projects. Break it down into smaller applications and complete one at a time. This prevents you from having to approach a big project in its entirety and possibly feeling overwhelmed. It's also a motivator for students to start early and not too late on class projects and assignments.

7. **A single project.** Students shouldn't set aside a day to study for multiple tests or complete multiple assignments. Work on them individually on different days, because it allows you to think on the individual assignment or project. If you are studying for a math exam but have a chemistry project awaiting your attention, you may rush to finish studying for the exam just to start working on the Chemistry project. This leads to insufficient attention being given to one or both subjects.

8. **Your study times should be short.** Don't get too excited. You still need to study efficiently in order to achieve positive results. This statement equates to students taking a break for 5-10 minutes after every hour of study time. This break serves as a brain booster in that it allows the student to clear their mind and regain focus before returning to the books.

9. **Get it done early.** Don't wait till late night to study. You're likely fatigued from the events and activities of the day by this time. Instead, study early on weekends and after school during the week. Review the principle schedule and agenda to ensure that you are on track and studying the right material for upcoming projects and exams. Night-time hours present an opportunity for more interruptions and temptations to nap, browse the web or spend time with friends or family.

10. **Sleep is an essential tool for students**. They need to get at least 8 or more hours of sleep each night. It helps them to feel more energized when they wake and improves their focus throughout the day. Circumstances may prevent this from happening every night but strive to do it at least 5 of the 7 nights in the week. If 8 hours isn't possible, at least get 6 or 7 hours of sleep to remain mentally and physically alert the next day. When you are sleep deprived, strive to set time aside for a nap during the day when you don't have other obligations. Most importantly, don't miss too much sleep because you can burn out or become fatigued. It could negatively impact your ability to concentrate, or score well on exams.

Are you a student and experiencing trouble with grades and staying on target? You are like many others who pursue a quality education. It's common, but it doesn't necessarily have to be challenging to be a quality student. Efficiently utilizing the time you have is a nice path to success for students. Making quality use of your time will allow you to set boundaries and set the pace for life after school. You will become a better person at work, in society and for those who depend on you if you are conscious of the time you have to get things done.

Students who work within preset time schedules find it easier to study and take tests. It's a cycle that must be continuously activated in order to experience quality results.

The Productive Student Cycle

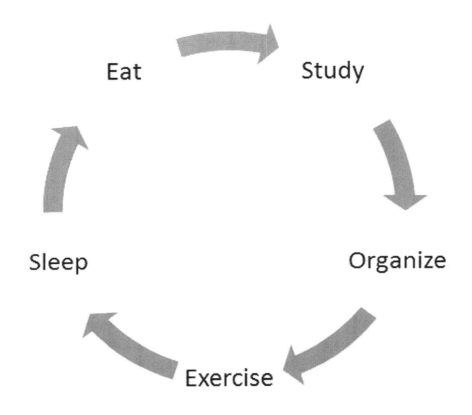

Eat

Study

Organize

Exercise

Sleep

The Social Life: Effective Time Management

You should know how important it is to make time for your social life. It keeps you healthy, happy, and helps you to perform well in other areas of life. You don't want to exhaust all your time on work, school, and family with nothing left to share in your social circle. Social time keeps you happy, energized, and in many ways, motivated. Allow enough time to experience quality relationships and activities that aren't required but preferred.

Imagine a round cake as a replica of your social life. Now, slice a piece for every person or thing that you want to devote a little time to. After it's all cut up, you could be left with only crumbs if you aren't managing your time properly. In every arrangement of your time, always allow time for self. Remember to take care of you, because no one else will have your best interest at heart when they are looking to spend time with you doing fun things or making memories. If you're overextended, you may find it difficult to enjoy the things you're scheduling yourself to do in your social circle.

The Social Life Breakdown

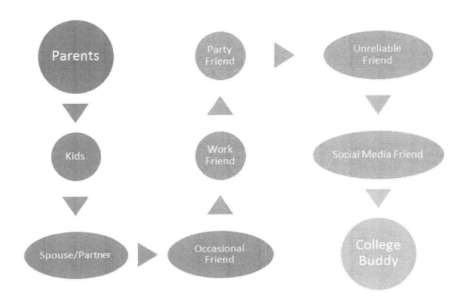

The breakdown of people that make up your social circle can be exhausting to think about. However, all these people have significant meaning to your life and contribute greatly to a large amount of the time you spend being social.

Are you managing your time properly in regards to your social circle? This is a pretty big group of people that you choose to give attention and time to. It's important to acknowledge and spend big moments with your peers and family in a social setting. Individuals should also be sure to utilize their time wisely and to stop robbing themselves of valuable time.

Remember this:

- Not every single person in your circle deserves time out of your schedule each day

- You can maintain quality relationships if you only see a person once per month or sometimes longer

- It's okay to mix friends from different walks of life into one time section

- Your spouse/partner and kids should not be treated like items on your schedule but should be considered valuable assets to your livelihood and happiness. Don't neglect time with them.

- Your spouse/partner and kids should not monopolize all of your time. It's okay to take a break away from them and have some alone time or time with friends.

- Your parents will always be your parents, call them, visit them, surprise them and set aside time to connect with them regularly if possible. You can learn a lot about managing life effectively from them. They have more experience than you do.

- Just because you have a great relationship with a co-worker, doesn't mean that relationship must exist outside the workplace. Keep work friends at work and limit the introductions to your outside circle.

- Your party friend may be too much of a party animal for you but you can still check on them often, grab lunch or a coffee with them when possible. Schedule things like workouts, walks in the park, or phone chats to stay connected and show you care.

- That friend from college has probably changed just as much as you have. Life goes on and you both or all have travelled different directions in life. Reconnect often, but not too often. Use social media or texts to keep each other informed of important milestones. Have an occasional reunion without the onset of guilt because you can't see one another on a consistent schedule.

- We all have that one friend who is completely unreliable but always relies on us to be there for them. Don't neglect that friend, but don't overextend yourself to their needs either. Give an occasional call or text to let them know you're thinking of them. Sometimes, you should wait a few hours or maybe a day before responding to their text or returning their call if it's not an emergency. This teaches them to value your time or not count on you to give them your time whenever they need it.

- What about the occasional friend? This is the friend that you don't see or hear from often but when you do, it's like you just saw them the day before. You both realize the importance of friendship and value each other's time. Send cards to say hello or texts just to check on them. These both require little time and can be managed effectively.

Negative Time Management Habits that Effect You Socially

- Setting appointment times too close together
- Scheduling multiple meetings on the same day
- Leaving home at the last minute and rushing through traffic to arrive on time
- Consistently cancelling meet-ups or appointments due to poor planning
- Waiting until the last minute to book travel arrangements
- Mixing up the time and day in the schedule for certain events

Positive Time Management Habits that Effect You Socially

- Planning ahead for important events
- Making a list of things that need to be done for the month
- Creating an email calendar to help you remember milestone events for friends and family
- Avoid last minute planning
- Engaging in activities that allow you to take time for yourself

Improve Negative Time Management Habits

You realize that your time management habits could use some improvement. For many, their goal is to get better each day with managing their time. It's not always as easy as saying that you'll do better. There must be strategies in place and a solid plan to help implement those strategies.

The benefits of improving your negative time management habits are tremendous. Life will seem to flow more efficiently and you'll begin to feel that you're more in touch with your wishes, and consider the needs of others when time management is implemented properly. Some people endure loads of stress because they are always running late, consistently missing appointments, and sometimes missing out on great opportunities due to poor management of time.

Don't live a life filled with regret, because you have no idea how to align your purpose with the time you have available. Learn how to apply the time you have to an essential rule in time management – regardless of the tasks awaiting you, you only get so many hours in a day. Stop worrying and stressing over the little things, and prepare properly for those important life tasks.

Tips to Fix Ineffective Time Management Practices

If you seek a better system of time management, you should be open to change. The biggest thing to realize is that there is no simple answer to the "why" behind your poor time management habits. You may have found by now that there are several methods that promise to help get you on track regarding time management. Some methods are efficient, while others are not so efficient.

Instead, a consistent and systematic approach will be more beneficial when attempting to make better use of your time. There are a few simple ways to reclaim your time and begin to enjoy life again. To begin, clarify the type of management habits you demonstrate. Move forward to break any negative habits that exist.

Review some familiar bad practices that occur with almost everyone. Here are a brief list and suggestions for efficient time management.

Procrastinator

This person has the most difficult time sticking to deadlines because they usually wait until the last minute to get things done. When asked, they usually answer that they're waiting on a good time to begin or until they are in a good mood. It is typical for them to underestimate the work requirements. For most procrastinators, they believe that they work better under high-pressure conditions. Procrastination can make things difficult for others also.

Overcoming the Habit

Procrastinators must learn to operate outside of reluctance to get things done. It is common for them to put their tasks off just because. Consider the amount of time needed to complete the task. Allow yourself plenty of time to bring the task to completion. You should know the purpose of each task you approach and remain focus during the completion phase. Complete the tasks for which you are most prepared first. It's not productive to begin a task that requires more time or equipment than you have available or access to.

Distracts Easily

If your attention span is short, your ability to focus will also be limited. This will cause you to lose focus on things that require your attention. Research shows that it's difficult for humans to concentrate on things for long periods at a time. This is true with tasks as well.

Advancements in technology are impairing our need to remain focused and impact various facets of life. If you are easily distracted, it will be hard to properly manage your time. Most often you won't complete tasks on time, due to consistent boredom and lack of productivity, which again, makes you miss important deadlines.

Overcoming the Habit

The best approach is to stop attempting to multi-task. The human brain has difficulties focusing in short spurts. If you are distracted easily, concentrate on completing a single job before you begin a new task. This allows you to avoid stress and not spread yourself too thin. It helps to restrict the use of mobile and technical devices to avoid distractions. Eliminate the temptation.

The Stickler for Getting It Right

Those who are determined to get everything right are meticulous and can take longer to complete projects because of this. Have you ever had a deadline that was reachable but because you take a long time to do certain things, you could easily miss the deadline. However, their level of high standards makes them critical of their own efforts and work. You will spend too much time on unessential details and fall behind on productivity. They have a hard time accepting help from others, which means it will take longer to complete the project alone.

The desire to do everything perfectly isn't a practical thought process.

Overcoming the Habit

For perfectionists, prioritize your tasks, and set a limitation on the length of time it should take for completion. If you are overwhelmed, analyze your actions to see if you have taken on too much. Some of the things are unnecessary and have no need to be added to the list. Assess the quality of your work and if it meets the standard, move on. Don't dwell on making things perfect.

Whatever you do, just get the job done.

Exercises to Improve Time Management

There are several exercises that work to help individuals or groups improve their time management efforts. Employing improvements in this area will help you to lead a more productive life as a student, employee, or as a person overall.

If you are serious about dedicating time and attention to getting on track with being productive and good with managing your time, these exercises are the ideal tool.

Consider these time management exercises.

1. The Mason Jar

This exercise teaches the significance of tackling important items on your list first. You will need an empty Mason jar, a few large stones, small stones, loose gravel, water, and dirt.

The order in which you place the items into the empty Mason jar effects the capacity of the space and the quantity of items you're able to put inside of it. For example, placing the dirt in first will fill the jar and make it difficult for much else to be placed inside the jar, other than water.

However, if you fill the jar first with the large stones, which represent those important items on your to-do list, and move on to the smaller items, which represent other things on the list, you will have an opportunity to place some of each item in the Mason jar.

2. Unknown Distractions

This is a great workplace exercise to improve time management. Split into groups that consist of at least two people. Each person in the group draws a name, which will be someone else in the group. Take turns demonstrating examples of ways that you've noticed the other person is distracted at work. If you pull a name of someone who is constantly on their phone, act that out and let others guess whose distraction you're acting out.

This exercise will help others to realize that they are distracted in ways they never imagined. You've identified your distractors, and can begin work on improving those areas.

3. Productivity Circle

You will need (3) 11x14 cardboards

Draw 24 circles on one side of each cardboard. On the first cardboard, write down the daily tasks that you complete at work. On the second, writer down those things you do while at work that are outside of your job duties. Now, Write the results from board 1 and board 2 on board 3. The number of unfilled circles represents your productivity levels.

4. The Arrangement

This exercise requires teams made up of (2-3) people and a deck of cards for each group.

One person acts as the host. Give each group specific instructions on the order in which their cards should be arranged. Hand the groups their deck of cards and set the timer to 1-minute. They have that long to get the cards arranged properly and according to the instructed order.

The objective is to get participants to collaborate, create a plan, and execute it within a set amount of time. It teaches proper planning and teaches you to manage your time more efficiently.

5. Get It Done

This exercise requires paper and pen.

Determine the size of the group by the number of participants you have. On each sheet of paper write a list of things-to-do, each worth a certain number of points. Give each group a list and tell them they have 15 minutes to complete their lists. At the end, calculate the points from each group. Have a discussion about how and why they chose to prioritize their list of things-to-do the way they did.

These are a few creative and easy to do exercises that can help you align your priorities and practice good time management.

How Bad Time Management Impacts Your Social Life

There are some individuals that enjoy being the center of the social circle. A large number of those individuals have horrible time management skills. It's not totally because they have no regard to the importance of their time or the time of others. Sometimes, they are consumed with the fun and joy of living life as a social bumble bee, and actually lose track of time. It may lead you to wonder if it's possible to properly manage time and enjoy a complete social life.

You will find that many people who enjoy the social scene are over or direct various social groups or host large events. You may now be wondering how they could possibly lead any type of social engagements if they are bad at managing their time. It's simple, they enjoy the social scene, and organize great events but typically recruit a strong team to assist with the planning. At least one member of the support team should be a stickler for good time management.

As a socially active person, it can be difficult to juggle a variety of engagements. Scheduling conflicts or invitations that counter time and date may happen often. With no intention, it's easy to accept more than one invitation to different events on the same day and at or near the same time. This type situation occurs common and the end-result is that you may miss or run late to an event for which you RSVP'd. While your intentions may be good, it still looks bad. Eventually, your name becomes a "maybe" in the invitation sector, when you're a habitual "no-show" type guest, you could possibly stop receiving invitations altogether.

If you have an extremely busy social life and receive multiple invitations, there are acceptable ways to decline the invite and remain in the good graces of the sender. Consider these options:

A. Send a reply stating that you are honored to have been invited but have a prior obligation.

B. Send a gift to arrive on the event date with a note expressing your regret for not making the event.

C. Send a digital card to acknowledge the occasion and inform of your inability to attend.

D. If appropriate, call or email the sender to acknowledge receipt of the invitation, and to explain that you will miss the occasion to which you were invited.

E. Instead of attempting to attend multiple events, choose one to attend and represent with a gift at the other.

These are a tiny few of the appropriate replies that help social bumble bees decline invitations. Understand that being sociable doesn't require you to be at every function or event that you're aware of or invited to. Your absence from a party, outing, or other celebration will be understood. It is also more acceptable than responding that you'll attend, only to later not show up or run late because you were entertaining multiple invitations. This is a main example of how good time management relies on good social mannerisms at times.

Good Time Management Practices for the Extremely Sociable

Juggling too many events isn't a bad problem to have, unless you lack the skills or tools to help you properly manage the required time to navigate your busy schedule. Exercising a healthy approach to the schedule is beneficial in holding you accountable for the management of your time.

Good time management practices are plentiful, but include measures like:

A. **Plan Ahead** – Failure to plan ahead can result in mismanagement of time. Develop a habit of preparing for the next week a few days ahead of its arrival. Make necessary travel arrangements soon before the planned date of travel. Map out your direction before you hit the road. These are proactive ways to stay ahead and not run behind on time whenever possible.

B. **Keep a Calendar** – Time is better managed when you have your upcoming events and special occasions written down. Keep calendars on your phone and other technical devices for easy access.

C. **Schedule Reminders** – Set reminder alerts on your calendar to ensure that you have proper time to prepare for the upcoming occasion.

The Social Time Management Pie

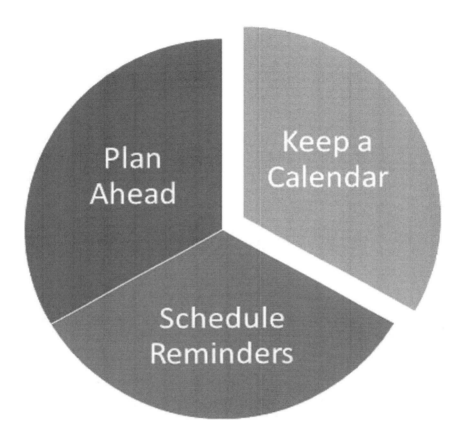

In addition to planning properly, it is essential to maintain mental clarity when trying to improve your time management habits. Your state of thinking could impact how effective you are in being on time for things you have scheduled.

These are the questions you should consider:

1. Do you suffer from brain fog?

2. Is it hard for you to make decisions without prolonged thought?

3. Are you constantly second-guessing your decisions?

4. Do you forget to plan for upcoming events and find yourself rushing at the last-minute?

If you answered yes to any of these questions, you will likely benefit from the mental clarity steps below.

Step 1: Prepare for productivity: exercise, eat right, and read inspirational or uplifting material

Step 2: Make a things-to-do list before bed: it helps you to wake-up knowing what you have on your agenda

Step 3: Get enough rest: make sure you get an efficient amount of rest. It helps you to maintain mental clarity and feel great the following day

Step 4: Rise early: don't lay in bed thinking of how you will approach your list of things to do. Rise at the sound of the alarm and complete your tasks.

Get Things Done and Live Life More Effectively

Do you sometimes feel that the more effort you give, the less efficient the results? As you take an assessment of your situation, you'll the things on your to-do list, it seems you're missing out on something. This is the feeling that many people have, even those who aren't perfectionist. You do as much as you can, but you still feel like you're not doing enough, right? Perhaps you even feel that you aren't enough for yourself or those around you. Could you be doing more, or is it that you're not making the most of what you're doing right now? The questions continue, but where are the answers?

You may be doing a lot, but not many of those things are the right things. It happens this way in many cases. You take on almost every task that comes your way, just to feel fulfilled. Consider this. You don't need to accept every task that comes your way. It's great that you want to do a lot, but how well are you doing those things?

- Does your schedule allow for such a large list of to-do items?

- Do you rush to complete a task, only to move on to the next?

- Are you sometimes less than satisfied with a particular task, but accept the outcome because you have other things to do?

- Do you feel that you need more hours in the day to accomplish your to-do list?

- Do you begin tasks but have a hard time completing them?

Are you aware that the more things you get done, the more effective your life will be? Your life doesn't have to feel incomplete because you have an increasing list of things that you desire to accomplish. The completion comes when you do things you have to do and still live an effective life. Manage your time and find the missing piece of your effectiveness.

Many times, people place greater pressure on themselves than others do. You feel that you'll let others down, people will see you differently, or you won't be good enough. These common fears are among the many that could possibly be interfering with your life being everything you need it to be.

You have the means, motive, and mentality. Now, it's time to get things done and live life more effectively. You have to know what an effective life is before you able to live it. In some cases, you must identify what makes life effective for you.

Life is Better When You Get Things Done on Time

Imagine being one of 20 or 30 students in a testing room and everyone completes the exam before you. Not only do they complete it before you, they finish with about 20 minutes remaining. Even worse, you're not quite finish when the timer sounds alerting the class that time is up. Now, what? More importantly, how do you feel? Those who finished early must really feel good about their results, as well as themselves.

It's understandable if you feel less than good. You maybe even feel a little let down. In essence, life is better when you get things done on time. Proper preparation and a solid time management system are likely tools utilized by the students that finished their test early. Does this mean that you should give up on being the best test-taker you can be? Not necessarily, it could mean that you need assistance in the area of test-preparation. This is an area where many people don't quite hit the mark. It's an area that if proper steps are taken, drastic improvements will be the result.

Are you one who gets things done consistently or are you struggling to get your timing on track? Take a look at this breakdown of why most people can't get things done consistently.

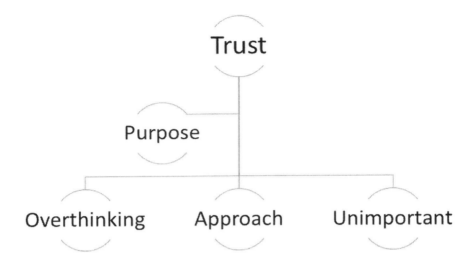

Trust

Purpose

Overthinking   Approach   Unimportant

Trust: Once you become familiar with doing things a certain way, it can be daunting to think about changing and trusting yourself to do it differently. It's not that you don't trust others. You don't trust yourself. Stop being so hard on yourself and trust that you'll learn the best steps regarding getting things done efficiently.

Purpose: What's the supporting purpose for what you're attempting to do? Is it crucial to you? If not, you won't be dedicated to doing the necessary things to achieve or accomplish it. The important things in life become the driving purpose in your life. Purpose is a primary motivator that keeps you working towards your goal. In life, it's important to know and understand your purpose.

Overthinking: Stop overthinking every single detail of what awaits you. Doing so can cause you to take too much time, get it wrong, and maybe not complete the task at all. You let time slip away when you are constantly thinking on how to do something or why something didn't work out before. Take the time you're wasting and start doing. Move in the best direction to get accomplish your tasks.

Approach: You are intimidate by tasks, concerned about upcoming deadlines, and yet you procrastinate when you have things to do. Instead, you focus on things around you that likely have no contributing effect on the task you have to do. If you are a procrastinator, approach the task slowly, by doing a bit at a time. Most importantly, keep a positive attitude about those things that you have awaiting you.

Unimportant: You are doing the unimportant things instead of focusing on what's important. Because it matters to you, it's obviously important but a few of the things on your list can probably be left off. Erase these and don't consider them as tasks, but add them to an "any day" list. These items can be done on any day and truly make no difference if you never get around to doing them.

Don't just read the list, if either or any of the things listed sound like something you're experiencing, do something about it. You will experience much more productivity in getting things done.

Why Am I Not Motivated?

A lack of motivation could also prevent you from getting things done. Do you wonder why you're not motivated enough to stay focused and finish your work or tasks on time to live life effectively? Okay, you may be tired on occasion, but this isn't the case every single time you need to get things done. Your life is unfulfilled because your motivation isn't where it should be, but once you figure out the "why", you can find the motivation you need.

If you seek motivation, step into it and live life more effectively. Motivation is something that gets you through the most challenging times. People that don't have challenges or encounter numerous obstacles are usually pretty motivated and pretty accomplished throughout their day.

Take these steps to get motivated, today!

Three Step Process to Getting Motivated

Check Your Surroundings: You can be experiencing a lack of motivation due to poor or negative surroundings. It could be your friends, coworkers, or clutter. Yes! All these factors make up your surroundings. You cannot become motivated or sustain motivation in a toxic environment.

Improve Your Surroundings: Once you've identified the negative elements that exist in your surroundings, remove them. Removing the factors that don't contribute to a motivated life is what you need to do next. Change your friends, or spend some time alone doing things that bring you joy. Avoid coworkers that don't respect your beliefs or interfere with your ability to be motivated in life. Also, if your home, workspace, and life in general is filled with clutter, it's time to declutter. Decluttering will increase your level of motivation.

Enjoy Your Surroundings: You've identified the negative factors and, improved your life by removing them. Now, you can begin enjoying your surroundings and living a good life. Excellent motivation encourages you to get things done on time and in the right way.

Other ways to feel motivated and inspired:

- Reading inspirational text

- Listening to motivational music

- Talking to positive people

- 'Taking weekend rides for the view or to visit someplace uplifting

- Speaking with those of whom you share similar interests

- Approaching and completing a project that at one time seemed unapproachable

- Connecting with distant friends or relatives with whom you've lost touch

Apply the previously listed motivational steps and suggestions to redirect the trajectory of your life. In doing so, ask yourself what could be changed to help you lead an effective life. The platform of your life is best supported by what makes you happy. It is common to allow the desires and requests of others to overshadow the things that motivate you to lead a more fulfilling lifestyle.

Happiness comes in various form and is different for

everyone. The things you put out and accept in life may be directly connected to how effective you are in life. Take a full assessment of your daily life and apply steps to feel better about where you are. The happiness you experience will dramatically impact your relationship with yourself and others. Most significantly, it helps you to accomplish more, make the most of your availability, and live a more effective life.

Visualization Performances to Enhance Your Happiness and Life

It may be difficult to imagine, but practicing certain visualization performances can help you embrace a happy life. In almost every situation, the point of happiness started as a vision or a dream. You must first imagine what you want and what it will bring to you before you process those wants into reality. Visualization has been an effective tool that when strategically applied can enhance your life. It assists in the enhancement of skill performance, creative techniques, emotional being, and goal achievements. Learning to acquire new skills or learn new habits should begin by first, imagining those desires inside your head.

The brain is designed to process future achievements, actions, and experiences by processing them visually. It's a natural process that happens without you being physically aware. It's very similar to breathing. You don't think about how important or vital it is to your life until you can't breathe properly.

Enhance your life, motivation and the belief in yourself with simulation. We've included essential visualization strategies that could enhance your mental, emotional, and physical happiness.

Here are suggested visualization strategies to consider.

Imagine and Define

Being able to clearly imagine something makes it

seem more realistic, which improves the brain's ability to establish a connection due to the repetitiveness of what's being imagined and the actual motivation you have to work towards your happiness. Here's something to consider. When you have been thinking about ice cream but suddenly stop thinking about it, you soon forget it was ever on your mind. But, if you think about that ice cream with eyes pierced shut, and think long and hard enough about it, the delicious toppings on your favorite flavor, that delicious taste, and zone in on the picture in your mind until you can taste the goodness in your mouth, you might immediately get up and go get that ice cream.

This is when the brain kicks into action mode to help you plan out the details of reaching the ultimate goal, getting the ice cream. You might consider where the closest place is to get it or the closest route to the store, or whether you have enough case in your purse to buy it. This is the process of creating little details that boost the eminence of your mental imitation, which requires utilization of all five senses. The more details you introduce into your visualization, the more realistic the process feels, which mimics the experience itself.

Sensitivity Intensification

Sensitivity is a form of sensory established depiction in the mind. Cognitive therapy informs us that sensitivity comes before thought. Once you can intensely feel a thing, you have encountered a certain belief connected to it. You have neutral feelings about things you know to be untrue, which permits you to watch or read fictional stories without having an impact on your emotions or sensitivity. But, you can believe something enough to make you feel that it's actually true, which could cause you to become sensitive about it.

Consider these strategies to help improve sensitivity intensification:

- Listen to calming music

- Sit in the dark with eyes closed

- Relax on a beach or at a spa with a clear mind

Disclosure

The mind produces what is stored, therefore it may be challenging to visualize a thing that you haven't actually experienced. It would be almost impossible to visualize yourself walking on the moon than it would to visualize yourself walking on a beach. To establish a specific and convincing visual representation mentally, you must have first been in that or a similar situation previously. Expose yourself to things that broaden your knowledge and cognizance of the experience. Visualization is a powerful process that produces powerful results. Embracing the creative abilities of the mind enables a process that helps you to see those things you wish to experience in real life.

Take the visualization strategies shown above and implement them to experience a sense of happiness you never thought possible. You may have been in acceptance of the way things are for so long that it's hard to imagine that you could be happier or living a more fulfilled life. Take the proper approach to visualize it correctly, and you can experience whatever you imagine in full form.

Exercises to Enhance Daily Living

Life may not always parallel what you imagined but you do have the ability to implement exercises that will enhance your daily living. Not to imply that your life is boring or less than suitable, but a realization that things could sometimes be better. Everyone desires to have a life of happiness, motivation, and maybe a little spontaneity from time to time. It's a simple and natural feeling that most people encounter in their lifetime.

Your desire may not be to change any one thing about your life, but only to enhance certain aspects of it. It's okay. You can admit this without guilt. Several people are withdrawn regarding this admission. They feel it's an admission of unhappiness, sadness, or a lack of fulfillment. It doesn't necessarily have to identify with either of these. As an individual, you are entitled to enhancement. You can enhance your looks, automobile, wardrobe and more. All these are forms of life enhancements.

Practices for Basic Life Enhancements in the:

HOME

1. Clear the Clutter
   o Clear out old magazines/brochures
   o Clear out old audio/video sets
   o Clear out old books
   o Clear out old small kitchen gadgets

2. Make this your mantra: every item has its home and there is a home for every item. Follow these guidelines to enforce this mantra:

   o Whoever removes it, returns it

   o Whoever dirties it, cleans it

   o Whoever tosses it down, retrieves it

   o Whoever pulls it off, put it up

3. Walk through the house and point out at least 50 things you tolerate. Commit to fix an item daily. Suggestions:

   o Dead batteries in a device

   o A stain in the carpet

   o An unorganized closet

   o Finish reading a book

   o Replace the broken door knob

CONTENTMENT

1. Jot down 3 to 4 things each day for which you are grateful.

2. Compile a list of things that you really like to do, and commit to do one or more each day for 45 consecutive days. Suggested things for the list:

   o Eating lunch away from your desk or the break room

   o Video calling a friend

   o Reading an excerpt of your favorite book

3. For five days, maintain a note of the talk that goes on inside your head, (good and bad). Be clear in your notes:

   o How often do you down yourself?

   o Do feelings of meagerness surface?

   o Are you critical of others?

   o How often do positive thoughts cross your mind?

   Write down how you feel when the thoughts occur. After the five days have passed and you've completed the above, make positive adjustments to your feelings by transforming the talk that takes place in your head.

4. For two consecutive months, laugh out loud daily. If you need motivation to laugh, find funny videos or memes online, or think of funny moments that occurred in the past.

PERSONAL GROWTH

1. Select a book, audio or paperback that you would need to really focus or concentrate to comprehend, and read a chapter or an excerpt per day. Adjust the daily reading to enable you to complete the book in one month.

2. Commit to acquire knowledge about something new daily. Something as meek as learning a new word and its definition or completely unimaginable, like something you've always had trouble doing. If you've reached your bedtime without learning a single new thing, open a digital translator and learn a word in a different language.

3. Make no complaints for 45 days or more. Complaints are directly related to negativity, which generates a negative mindset. It's important to stop yourself from complaining and if you catch yourself doing it, STOP immediately.

4. Schedule your alarm to sound off 60 seconds earlier each day for the upcoming 90 days. Spring out of bed the moment the alarm sets off. Pull back the curtains, or open your blinds to feel the direct sunlight. Do yoga or meditate, if you prefer. After three months, you'll be rising one and a half hour earlier than you are now.

5. Write morning affirmations for 90 consecutive days. This is done by drafting long-form notes during your morning routine, before departing home.

6. Commit to think of words and pictures that define or are aligned with the desires of your life. Who do you see yourself being, and how are you different than what you imagined? What are motivational factors in your life? What are you aiming to achieve? The answers to these questions should be associated with the images you visualize in your mind.

FINANCES

1. Map out a budget. Be sure to account for each dollar spent for three months to ensure you're staying within your budget.

2. Research to find tips on being economical. Choose eight tips and apply them to your process for the three months that you maintain the budget. Consider:

   o Going shopping with no debit or credit cards, but cash instead.

   o Make a detailed shopping list before leaving home and do not purchase anything not listed.

   o Decrease your cable bill or cut it altogether.

   o Say goodbye to your home phone if you have one. Your mobile line is the more beneficial of the two.

   o Make a list of errands and run them all at single time during the week.

   Take a note of the amount of money you were able to save by employing these tips.

3. For three months, pay for everything using paper money only. Store any change you receive in the form of coins in a container. Once time has passed, count the coins to determine the amount you were able to save.

4. For 90 days, if it's not a necessity, don't purchase it. Money saved using this exercise should go towards:

   o Paying towards your existing debt

   o Establishing or increasing your emergency account

   o Investments or savings

5. For 90 consecutive days, designate an hour to create a source of additional income.

TIME MANAGEMENT

1. For 90 days, keep a notebook on your person wherever you go. Utilize this to keep an accurate account of your occurring thoughts. Anything that you may ponder or possibly think that you need to do, things that bother you, things that you need to recall later, or mimicking thoughts should be listed in this notebook. It's your clutter companion, because it holds all the clutter than clogs your brain. Suggestions of things to record:

    o Ideas for projects

    o Important dates

    o Appointments

    o Task list

2. For a full week, keep a note of how your time is spent. At week's end, review the list to assess the areas of which your availability could be better managed. You should create a budget for your time also. It's possible to spend too much time on all the wrong things. Things that may need addressing include:

    o Chores

    o Socializing

    o Work related activities

    o Traveling

    Be sure to adhere to your budget for three months.

3. Designate a single minute activity that you can omit from your schedule for the next three months, and assign that time to high-priority activities.

4. Pinpoint five areas where you often misuse time, restrict the time you spend daily doing these things for the next three months. Examples are:

   o Watch an hour less of television than you usually do each day.

   o Spend a maximum of one hour each day on social media

   o Spend thirty minutes or less on your game platform each day

5. For three consecutive months, focus on doing one thing without being distracted, and no multi-tasking allowed.

6. For 90 consecutive days, complete the high-priority items on your tasks list first.

7. Over the next three months, carefully evaluate your progress of each week. During the evaluation, answer these questions:

   o What, if anything were you able to achieve?

   o What challenges were met?

   o What were the pros?

8. Over the next three months, spend time daily cleaning or reorganizing your work space, filing old papers, and ensuring that your workspace is decluttered. This permits you to have access to a clean workspace daily.

9. List out each event or social engagement that is scheduled for the next three to four months. With a marker or pen, strike through any item that doesn't make you happy or feel pleased to attend or participate in. This is a process of determining what things in life are really important to your happiness.

Living an effective life depends greatly on your perception of effective. For some, it takes a lot to make them feel that life is effective. For others, it only takes the minimum. Whatever you feel is necessary to help you experience maximum effectiveness in life, go for it. It can be motivational to experience something different with each day. The feeling of not knowing what to expect is one that generates excitement and positive thoughts.

You have been given efficient practices, steps and suggestions to get things done in quality time in order to generate positive results, such as living an effective daily life. Applied as suggested, all these tools can contribute to the mental and emotional happiness you experience in life.

Productivity Planner

The following productivity planner is to assist in the planning of your week.

Add your tasks to the bullet points for each day of the week.

You may choose to color code the tasks by highlighting according to the category (Red for priority, Green for work related, Blue for miscellaneous)

Once a task is completed, delete it to begin the next week with a clear productivity tasks

If a task remains undone for a couple weeks, reassess the importance of it to see if it should remain on the planner or be moved to a project list.

Day	Priority	Work	Miscellaneous	Recovery
Monday				
Tuesday				
Wednesday				
Thursday				
Friday				
Saturday				
Sunday				

Imprint

Peter L. Gardner proxy of:
EnvDur Trading
BalatMahallesi Rifat
Efendi Sokak, No: 19/1
34087 Istanbul
Turkey

Design: Alima Media Turk
Picture: Liliya Kandrashevich

Printed in Great Britain
by Amazon